Especially for

_____

From

_____

Date

_____

© 2010 by Barbour Publishing, Inc.

Compiled by Kathy Shutt.

ISBN 978-1-60260-824-5

Scripture quotations marked NASB are taken from the New American Standard Bible, © 1960, 1962, 1963, 1968, 1971, 1972, 1973, 1975, 1977, 1995 by The Lockman Foundation. Used by permission.

Scripture quotations marked NLT are taken from the *Holy Bible*, New Living Translation, copyright © 1996, 2004. Used by permission of Tyndale House Publishers, Inc. Wheaton, Illinois 60189, U.S.A. All rights reserved.

Scripture quotations marked KJV are taken from the King James Version of the Bible.

Scripture quotations marked NIV are taken from the HOLY BIBLE, NEW INTERNATIONAL VERSION®. NIV®. Copyright © 1973, 1978, 1984 by International Bible Society. Used by permission of Zondervan. All rights reserved.

Prayers are taken from *365 Prayers for Women* and *365 Everyday Prayers*, published by Barbour Publishing, Inc.

Published by Barbour Publishing, Inc., P.O. Box 719, Uhrichsville, Ohio 44683, www.barbourbooks.com

Our mission is to publish and distribute inspirational products offering exceptional value and biblical encouragement to the masses.

Member of the
Evangelical Christian
Publishers Association

Printed in China.

365
Inspiring Thoughts
for Grandmothers

BARBOUR
PUBLISHING

Grandmas Are For...

Grandmas are for stories
about things of long ago.
Grandmas are for caring
about all the things you know.
Grandmas are for rocking you
and singing you to sleep.
Grandmas are for giving you
nice memories to keep.
Grandmas are for knowing
all the things you're dreaming of.
But, most of all, grandmas are for love.

— UNKNOWN

DAY 2

One Heart...

If I can stop one heart from breaking,
I shall not love in vain;
If I can ease one life the aching,
or cool one pain...
I shall not live in vain.

—EMILY DICKINSON

DAY 3

Nothing Is Wasted

Nothing you do for children is ever
wasted. They seem not to notice us,
hovering, averting our eyes, and they
seldom offer thanks, but what we do for
them is never wasted.

—GARRISON KEILLOR

Do Good

Do all the good you can, by all the means you can,
in all the ways you can, in all the places you can,
at all the times you can, to all the people you can,
as long as ever you can.

—JOHN WESLEY

Chain of Love

Grandparents bestow upon their grandchildren the strength and wisdom that time and experience have given them. Grandchildren bless their grandparents with a youthful vitality and innocence that help them stay young at heart forever. Together they create a chain of love linking the past with the future. The chain may strengthen, but it will never part.

—Unknown

DAY 6

Endless Good

We walk without fear, full of hope and courage and
strength to do [God's] will, waiting for the endless
good which He is always giving as fast as He can
get us to take it in.

—GEORGE MACDONALD

DAY 7

By the Grace of God

I am only one, but I am one. I can't do
everything, but I can do something.
And what I can do, that I ought to do.
And what I ought to do, by the grace
of God, I shall do.

—EDWARD E. HALE

DAY 8

Faith

Sight is not faith, and hearing is not faith,
neither is feeling faith, but believing when we
neither see, hear, nor feel is faith;
and everywhere the Bible tells us our salvation is
to be by faith. Therefore we must believe before
we feel, and often against our feelings,
if we would honor God by our faith.

—HANNAH WHITALL SMITH

DAY 9

A Steadfast Heart

Give me, O Lord, a steadfast heart,
which no unworthy affection may drag
downwards; give me an unconquered
heart, which no tribulation can wear out;
give me an upright heart, which no
unworthy purpose may tempt aside.

—St. Thomas Aquinas

No One Can Take the Place of Grandma!

Who better to sit down with and enjoy a hot fudge sundae and a lot of giggles? Grandmas are true friends for life. Nowhere else can you find such a friend.

- Grandmas never hold a grudge
- Grandmas love to listen to your stories
- Grandmas share your hopes and dreams

In all the world, no one can take the place of a grandma!

—K. WILLIAMS

Love

Love is the key. Joy is love singing.
Peace is love resting. Long-suffering is
love enduring. Kindness is love's touch.
Goodness is love's character.
Faithfulness is love's habit. Gentleness is
love's self-forgetfulness. Self-control is
love holding the reins.

—DONALD GREY BARNHOUSE

Actions

We won't always know whose lives we touched and
made better for our having cared, because actions
can sometimes have unforeseen ramifications.
What's important is that you do care and you act.

—CHARLOTTE LUNDSFORD

Like a Garden

Your family and your love must be
cultivated like a garden. Time, effort,
and imagination must be summoned
constantly to keep any relationship
flourishing and growing.

—JIM ROHN

Brave Enthusiasm

A young child is, indeed, a true scientist,
just one big question mark. What? Why? How?
I never cease to marvel at the recurring miracle
of growth, to be fascinated by the mystery and
wonder of this brave enthusiasm.

—VICTORIA WAGNER

Love Never Fails

Love is patient, love is kind. It does not
envy, it does not boast, it is not proud.
It is not rude, it is not self-seeking,
it is not easily angered, it keeps no record
of wrongs. Love does not delight in evil
but rejoices with the truth. It always
protects, always trusts, always hopes,
always perseveres. Love never fails.

—1 CORINTHIANS 13:4–8 NIV

Acceptance

Our grandchildren accept us for ourselves, without
rebuke or effort to change us, as no one in our entire
lives has ever done, not our parents, siblings, spouses,
friends—and hardly ever our grown children.

—RUTH GOODE

A Choice

Happiness in the older years of life, like happiness in every year of life, is a matter of choice—your choice for yourself.

—HAROLD AZINE

Best Harvest

Your best harvest may be the pleasure you get from working with family and friends. There's never a shortage of things to do, no limit to the lessons that can be learned.

—STEVEN WILLSON

Happy Chance

We are not the same persons this year as
last; nor are those we love. It is a happy
chance if we, changing, continue to love
a changed person.

—W. Somerset Maugham

Beautifully Adorned

O Father, You have draped me in the
garments of salvation and wrapped me snugly
in the robe of righteousness. I am beautifully
adorned by You—for You. You have given me
all I need to live a joyful life, and I rejoice in
Your gifts of beauty. Amen.

Hilarious Heritage

I refer to my grandchildren as my
"hilarious heritage." As one of them once
told me, they keep me "giggled up."
I love being around them because they
are so funny.

—CONOVER SWOFFORD

Heirlooms

To our grandchildren, we are the owners of heirlooms and the source of their history. . .soft pillows, home-baked cookies, and the hoarse voice after ball games. . . . We are the playmates who offer security, help with chores, give second opinions (unbiased), and can read nine books aloud at a sitting.

—C. Ellen Watts

I Am

I am not what I ought to be. I am not
what I wish to be. I am not even what I
hope to be. But by the cross of Christ,
I am not what I was.

—John Newton

God's Glory

All God's glory and beauty come from within,
and there He delights to dwell. His visits there are
frequent, His conversations sweet, His comforts
refreshing, His peace passing all understanding.

—THOMAS À KEMPIS

Newly Created

And if tonight my soul may find her
peace in sleep, and sink in good oblivion,
and in the morning wake like a
new-opened flower, then I have been
dipped again in God, and new-created.

—D.H. LAWRENCE

Radiance

I don't believe makeup and the right hairstyle
alone can make a woman beautiful.
The most radiant woman in the room is the
one full of life and experience.

—UNKNOWN

Spirit of Love

You will find as you look back upon your
life that the moments when you have
truly lived are the moments when you
have done things in the spirit of love.

—HENRY DRUMMOND

DAY 28

A Forever Friend

Sometimes in life, you find a special friend.
Someone who changes your life just by being a
part of it. Someone who makes you laugh until
you can't stop. Someone who makes you believe
that there is good in the world. Someone who
convinces you that there really is an unlocked door
just waiting for you to open it.
This is forever friendship.

—Unknown

God's Work

To be a joy-bearer and a joy-giver says everything, for in our life, if one is joyful, it means that one is faithfully living for God, and that nothing else counts; and if one gives joy to others, one is doing God's work.

—JANET ERSKINE STUART

Secret Things

The secret things belong to the LORD our God,
but the things revealed belong to us and to our
children forever, that we may follow all the words
of this law.

—DEUTERONOMY 29:29 NIV

The Game of Life

Whether sixty or sixteen, there is in every human being's heart the love of wonder; the sweet amazement at the stars and starlike things, the undaunted challenge of events, the unfailing childlike appetite for what-next, and the joy of the game of living.

—SAMUEL ULLMAN

DAY 32

Heart's Gratitude

As flowers carry dewdrops, trembling on the
edges of the petals and ready to fall at the first
waft of the wind or brush of bird, so the heart
should carry its beaded words of thanksgiving.
At the first breath of heavenly flavor,
let down the shower, perfumed with
the heart's gratitude.

—HENRY WARD BEECHER

What a Friend We Have in Jesus

What a friend we have in Jesus,
all our sins and griefs to bear!
What a privilege to carry
everything to God in prayer!
O what peace we often forfeit,
O what needless pain we bear,
All because we do not carry
everything to God in prayer.

—JOSEPH M. SCRIVEN

O Happy Home

O happy home, where Thou art loved the dearest,
  Thou loving Friend and Savior of our race,
And where among the guests there never cometh
  One who can hold such high and honored place!

—KARL J. SPITTA

Let the Children Come to Me

When Jesus Christ asked the little
children to come to Him, He didn't say
only rich children, or white children,
or children with two-parent families,
or children who didn't have a mental or
physical handicap. He said,
"Let *all* children come to Me."

—MARIAN WRIGHT EDELMAN

DAY 36

From This Day On...

I have resolved that from this day on, I will do all
the business I can honestly, have all the fun I can
reasonably, do all the good I can willingly, and save
my digestion by thinking pleasantly.

—ROBERT LOUIS STEVENSON

DAY 37

Lessons of an Oyster

The most extraordinary thing about the
oyster is this. Irritations get into his shell.
He does not like them. But. . .he uses
the irritation to do the loveliest thing an
oyster ever has a chance to do. If there are
irritations in our lives today, there is only
one prescription: Make a pearl. It may
have to be a pearl of patience. . . .
And it takes faith and love to do it.

—HARRY EMERSON FOSDICK

Prayer and Pains

We must not sit still and look for miracles;
up and doing, and the Lord will be with thee.
Prayer and pains, through faith in Christ Jesus,
will do anything.

—GEORGE ELIOT

Stardust

Nobody can do for little children what
grandparents can do. Grandparents sort
of sprinkle stardust over the lives of
little children.

—ALEX HALEY

I Am Loved

I tell You my problems and You listen, Lord.
I speak of the good things in my life and You smile.
I ask You for advice, knowing it will come in Your
time. I am no longer lonely; I am loved. Amen.

DAY 41

Bless This Life

O Thou who dwellest in so many homes,
possess Thyself of this. Bless the life that
is sheltered here. Grant that trust and
peace and comfort abide within, and that
love and life and usefulness may go out
from this home forever.

—UNKNOWN

DAY 42

What Is Love?

Love. What is love?
No one can define it;
It's something so great,
Only God could design it.
Yes, love is beyond what man can define,
For love is immortal, and God's gift is divine.

—UNKNOWN

Abide in Him

Let other things come and go as they may,
let other people criticize as they will,
but never allow anything to obscure the
life that is hid with Christ in God.
Never be hurried out of the relationship
of abiding in Him.

—OSWALD CHAMBERS

Happiness Depends on Your Disposition

I am still determined to be cheerful and happy, in whatever situation I may be; for I also have learned from experience that the greater part of our happiness or misery depends upon our dispositions, and not on our circumstances.

—MARTHA WASHINGTON

Everlasting Mercy

But the mercy of the LORD is from
everlasting to everlasting upon them that
fear him, and his righteousness unto
children's children.

—Psalm 103:17 KJV

A Child's Hand

A child's hand in yours—what tenderness it
arouses, what power it conjures. You are instantly
the very touchstone of wisdom and strength.

—Marjorie Holmes

I Am the Vine

I am the vine, you are the branches;
he who abides in Me and I in him,
he bears much fruit, for apart from Me
you can do nothing.

—John 15:5 NASB

Take My Life and Let It Be

Take my life and let it be
consecrated, Lord, to Thee.
Take my moments and my days;
let them flow in ceaseless praise.
Take my hands, and let them move
at the impulse of Thy love.
Take my feet, and let them be
swift and beautiful for Thee.

—FRANCES R. HAVERGAL

Your Heart's Desire

May you always have walls for the winds,
a roof for the rain, tea beside the fire,
laughter to cheer you, those you love near
you, and all your heart might desire.

—IRISH BLESSING

Success

Success does not necessarily mean that
we must earn a great deal of money and live
in the biggest house in town. It means only
that we are daily engaged in striving toward a
goal that we have independently chosen and
feel is worthy of us as persons. A goal, whatever
it may be, is what gives meaning to our
existence. It is the carrot on the stick that
keeps us striving—that gives us a reason
for getting out of bed in the morning.

—Reader's Digest

DAY 51

Basic Substance of Life

The here, the now, and the individual
have always been the special concern of
the saint, the artist, the poet—and from
time immemorial—the woman.
In the small circle of home she has never
quite forgotten the particular uniqueness
of each member of the family;
the spontaneity of now; the vividness of
here. This is the basic substance of life.

—ANNE MORROW LINDBERGH

Good Character

Good character is more to be praised than
outstanding talent. Most talents are to some extent
a gift. Good character, by contrast, is not given to
us. We have to build it piece by piece by thought,
choice, courage, and determination.

—JOHN LUTHER

DAY 53

The Greatest Blessing

The Bible is one of the greatest blessings
bestowed by God upon the children of
men. It has God for its author, salvation
for its end, and truth without any mixture
for its matter. It is all pure, all sincere;
nothing too much; nothing wanting.

—JOHN LOCKE

Patience, Acceptance, and Contentment

It is in the everyday and commonplace that we learn patience, acceptance, and contentment.

—RICHARD J. FOSTER

Some Good Thing

At some time in our life we feel a
trembling, fearful longing to do some
good thing. Life finds its noblest spring
of excellence in this hidden impulse
to do our best.

—ROBERT COLLYER

Sleep in Peace

Have courage for the great sorrows of life and
patience for the small ones; and when you have
laboriously accomplished your daily task,
go to sleep in peace. God is awake.

—VICTOR HUGO

What Love Looks Like

What does it look like? It has hands to
help others, feet to hasten to the poor and
needy, eyes to see misery and want, ears to
hear the sighs and sorrows of men.
That is what love looks like.

—St. Augustine

Pass It On

Have you had a kindness shown?
Pass it on;
'Twas not given for thee alone,
Pass it on;
Let it travel down the years,
Let it wipe another's tears,
Till in heaven the deed appears,
Pass it on.

—HENRY BURTON

A Little Bit...

A grandmother is a little bit parent,
a little bit teacher,
and a little bit best friend.

—Unknown

DAY 60

Choose Life

Therefore choose life, that both thou and thy seed
may live: That thou mayest love the LORD thy God,
and that thou mayest obey his voice, and that thou
mayest cleave unto him: for he is thy life,
and the length of thy days.

—DEUTERONOMY 30:19–20 KJV

A Nurturing Family

Feelings of worth can flourish only in an
atmosphere where individual differences
are appreciated, mistakes are tolerated,
communication is open, and rules are
flexible—the kind of atmosphere that is
found in a nurturing family.

—VIRGINIA SATIR

The Best Thing

The best thing to give your enemy is
forgiveness; to an opponent, tolerance;
to a friend; your heart; to your child,
a good example; to a father, deference; to your
mother, conduct that will make her proud of
you; to yourself, respect; to all men, charity.

—FRANCIS MAITLAND BALFOUR

DAY 63

We Are God's

We are consecrated and dedicated to
God; therefore we may not hereafter
think, speak, meditate, or do anything but
with a view to His glory. We are God's;
to Him therefore, let us live and die.

—JOHN CALVIN

Renewal

By reading the scriptures I am so renewed that all
nature seems renewed around me and with me.
The sky seems to be a pure, cooler blue, the trees a
deeper green. . . . The whole world is charged with
the glory of God and I feel fire and music. . .
under my feet.

—THOMAS MERTON

DAY 65

Godly Women

I am convinced that the influence
of an army of godly women will be
incalculable—in our homes,
our churches, and our culture.
Will you be one of those women?

—Nancy Leigh DeMoss

Sweet Hour of Prayer

Sweet hour of prayer! Sweet hour of prayer!
The joys I feel, the bliss I share,
of those whose anxious spirits burn
with strong desires for thy return!
With such I hasten to the place
where God my Savior shows His face,
and gladly take my station there,
and wait for thee, sweet hour of prayer!

—WILLIAM WALFORD

How Far Will You Go?

How far you go in life depends on
your being tender with the young,
compassionate with the aged,
sympathetic with the striving,
and tolerant of the weak and strong.
Because someday in life,
you will have been all of these.

—GEORGE WASHINGTON CARVER

A Grandma Is Perfection

Truth be told, being a grandma is as close as we ever get to perfection. The ultimate warm sticky bun with plump raisins and nuts. Clouds nine, ten, and eleven.

—Bryna Nelson Paston

DAY 69

Birth of a Grandchild

The birth of a grandchild is a wonderful
and exciting event! That wonder and
excitement continues throughout life.

—TOM POTTS

DAY 70

Coming into Grace

It is as grandmothers that our mothers come into
the fullness of their grace.

—CHRISTOPHER MORLEY

You Are Never Alone

Father, when troubles come, I never have
to face them alone. Thank You for always
being with me as my refuge and strength.
When all else fails, I put my trust in You
and am never disappointed. Amen.

The Standard of Faith

It is a masterpiece of the devil to make us believe
that children cannot understand religion.
Would Christ have made a child the standard of
faith if He had known that it was not capable of
understanding His words?

—DWIGHT L. MOODY

Tell Me a Story

Grandma and Grandpa, tell me a story
and snuggle me with your love. When I'm
in your arms, the world seems small and
we're blessed by the heavens above.

—LAURA SPIESS

God Has Done It All

If I could give you information of my life, it would be to show how a woman of very ordinary ability has been led by God in strange and unaccustomed paths to do in His service what He has done in her. And if I could tell you all, you would see how God has done all, and I nothing. I have worked hard, very hard, that is all; and I have never refused God anything.

—FLORENCE NIGHTINGALE

DAY 75

Everlasting Life

For God so loved the world, that he gave
his only begotten Son, that whosoever
believeth in him should not perish,
but have everlasting life.

—JOHN 3:16 KJV

Character Counts

A sound body is a first-class thing; a sound mind
is an even better thing; but the thing that counts
for most in the individual, as in the nation,
is character, the sum of those qualities which make
a man a good man and a woman a good woman.

—THEODORE ROOSEVELT

Asking for Nothing

We are women, and my plea is,
Let me be a woman, holy through and
through, asking for nothing but what God
wants to give me, receiving with both hands
and with all my heart whatever that is.

—ELISABETH ELLIOT

Christian Service

The most eloquent prayer is the prayer through hands that heal and bless. The highest form of worship is the worship of unselfish Christian service. The greatest form of praise is the sound of consecrated feet seeking out the lost and helpless.

—BILLY GRAHAM

Longevity

A man ninety years old was asked to what he attributed his longevity. "I reckon," he said, with a twinkle in his eye, "it's because most nights I went to bed and slept when I should have stayed up and worried."

—GARSON KANIN

DAY 80

My Jesus, I Love Thee

My Jesus, I love Thee, I know Thou art mine;
For Thee all the follies of sin I resign.
My gracious Redeemer, my Savior art Thou;
If ever I loved Thee, my Jesus, 'tis now.

—WILLIAM R. FEATHERSTON

DAY 81

Share Love

Love cannot remain by itself—it has no meaning. Love has to be put into action, and that action is service. Whatever form we are, able or disabled, rich or poor, it is not how much we do, but how much love we put in the doing; a lifelong sharing of love with others.

—MOTHER TERESA

The World

The world is not respectable; it is mortal,
tormented, confused, deluded forever; but it is
shot through with beauty, with love, with glints of
courage and laughter; and in these, the spirit blooms
timidly and struggles to the light amid the thorns.

—GEORGE SANTAYANA

Christ Is an Example

In His life, Christ is an example, showing
us how to live; in His death, He is a
sacrifice, satisfying for our sins;
in His resurrection, a conqueror;
in His ascension, a king;
in His intercession, a high priest.

—MARTIN LUTHER

Woven into Jesus

God will never, never, never let us down if we have
faith and put our trust in Him. He will always look
after us. So we must cleave to Jesus. Our whole life
must simply be woven into Jesus.

—MOTHER TERESA

Fill Me

Lord, I give up all my own purposes and plans, all my own desires and hopes and ambitions and accept Thy will for my life. I give myself, my life, my all, utterly to Thee, to be Thine forever. I hand over to Thy keeping all my friendships; all the people whom I love are to take a second place in my heart. Fill me and seal me with Thy Holy Spirit. Work out Thy whole will in my life—at any cost— now and forever.

—Betty Stam

My Savior Leads Me

All the way my Savior leads me;
What have I to ask beside?
Can I doubt His tender mercy,
Who through life has been my Guide?
Heav'nly peace, divinest comfort,
Here by faith in Him to dwell!
For I know, whate'er befall me,
Jesus doeth all things well;
For I know, whate'er befall me,
Jesus doeth all things well.

—FANNY CROSBY

We Never Grow Old

People like you and I, though mortal of
course like everyone else, do not grow old
no matter how long we live. . . .
[We] never cease to stand like curious
children before the great mystery
into which we were born.

—ALBERT EINSTEIN

Live with Honor

The shortest and surest way to live with honor in the world is to be in reality what we would appear to be; and if we observe, we shall find that all human virtues increase and strengthen themselves by the practice and experience of them.

—SOCRATES

Nourish Children

To nourish children and raise them
against odds is in any time, any place,
more valuable than to fix bolts in cars or
design nuclear weapons.

—MARILYN FRENCH

The Fullness of Time

But when the fulness of the time was come,
God sent forth his Son, made of a woman,
made under the law, to redeem them that were under
the law, that we might receive the adoption of sons.

—GALATIANS 4:4–5 KJV

My House

Lord, I want my house to be Your house—a house of prayer, a place of comfort and peace, a refuge to those in need. Help me make our home a blessing for all who pass through its door. Amen.

God's Word

So great is my veneration for the Bible,
that the earlier my children begin to read it
the more confident will be my hopes that they
will prove useful citizens to their country and
respectable members of society.

—JOHN QUINCY ADAMS

Cheerful

A cheerful temper joined with innocence
will make beauty attractive,
knowledge delightful, and wit
good-natured. It will lighten sickness,
poverty, and affliction; convert ignorance
into an amiable simplicity, and render
deformity itself agreeable.

—JOSEPH ADDISON

Direct Me

O most glorious God, in Jesus Christ. . .
Let me live according to those holy rules which
Thou hast this day prescribed in Thy holy Word. . . .
Direct me to the true object, Jesus Christ:
the way, the truth, and the life. Bless, O Lord,
all the people of this land.

—GEORGE WASHINGTON

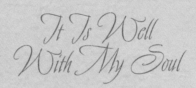

It Is Well With My Soul

And Lord, haste the day
when my faith shall be sight,
The clouds be rolled back as a scroll;
The trump shall resound,
and the Lord shall descend,
Even so, it is well with my soul.

—HORATIO G. SPAFFORD

Friends

It is great to have friends when one is young,
but indeed it is still more so when you are
getting old. When we are young, friends are, like
everything else, a matter of course. In the old days,
we know what it means to have them.

—EDVARD GRIEG

Wonderful Blessings of Age

You get to be silly and people think
you're cute. You get to appreciate more,
remember less, and realize how good they
both can be. You get to move slowly.
You get to see the world through the eyes
of wisdom. You get to believe that your
life revolves around your friends. . .and
when you get to see them again.

—BONNIE JENSEN

Blessings Unaware

The lives that have been the greatest blessing
to you are the lives of those people who
themselves were unaware of having
been a blessing.

—OSWALD CHAMBERS

All Good Things

Fear less, hope more;
Eat less, chew more;
Whine less, breath more;
Talk less, say more;
Love more,
And all good things will be yours.

—SWEDISH PROVERB

Best Things in the World

The best and most beautiful things in the world
cannot be seen or even touched.
They must be felt with the heart.

—HELEN KELLER

What Is a Friend?

A friend is one to whom one may pour
out all the contents of one's heart,
chaff and grain together, knowing that
the gentlest of hands will take and sift
it, keep what is worth keeping and with a
breath of kindness blow the rest away.

—ARABIAN PROVERB

Footprints

Life is full of people who will make you laugh, cry,
smile until your face hurts, and so happy that you
think you'll burst. But the ones who leave their
footprints on your soul are the ones
that keep your life going.

—NATALIE BERNOT

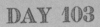

An Irish Blessing

May there always be work for your hands to do. May your purse always hold a coin or two. May the sun always shine on your windowpane. May a rainbow be certain to follow each rain. May the hand of a friend always be near you. May God fill your heart with gladness to cheer you.

DAY 104

*Spring
Will Come!*

Even in winter, even in the midst of the
storm, the sun is still there. Somewhere,
up above the clouds, it still shines and warms
and pulls at the life buried deep inside the
brown branches and frozen earth. The sun is
there! Spring will come! The clouds cannot
stay forever.

—GLORIA GAITHER

Run the Race

Wherefore seeing we also are compassed
about with so great a cloud of witnesses,
let us lay aside every weight, and the sin
which doth so easily beset us, and let
us run with patience the race that is set
before us, looking unto Jesus the author
and finisher of our faith.

—HEBREWS 12:1–2 KJV

Invincible

Joy is the holy fire that keeps our purpose warm
and our intelligence aglow. Work without joy is
nothing. Resolve to keep happy, and your joy and
you shall form an invincible host
against difficulties.

—HELEN KELLER

To Believe

To believe in God for me is to feel that there is a God, not a dead one or a stuffed one, but a living one, who with irresistible force urges us toward more loving.

—VINCENT VAN GOGH

Everything

When I stand before God at the end of my life,
I would hope that I would not have a single bit
of talent left and could say, "I used everything
You gave me."

—ERMA BOMBECK

Satisfaction

Look at a day when you are supremely
satisfied at the end. It is not a day when
you lounge around doing nothing; it is
when you have had everything to do,
and you have done it.

—MARGARET THATCHER

Happiness Is . . .

Happiness is a butterfly, which, when pursued,
is always beyond our grasp, but which, if you will
sit down quietly, may alight upon you.

—NATHANIEL HAWTHORNE

DAY 111

Sweetest Joys

Friendship is one of the sweetest joys
in life. Many might have failed beneath
the bitterness of their trial had they not
found a friend.

—CHARLES SPURGEON

Heavenly Fire

There is in every true woman's heart a spark of
heavenly fire, which lies dormant in the broad
daylight of prosperity, but which kindles up and
beams and blazes in the dark hour of adversity.

—WASHINGTON IRVING

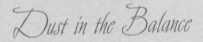

Dust in the Balance

All the joy and delight, all the pleasures
a thousand worlds could offer, are as dust
in the balance when weighed against one
hour of this mutual exchange of love and
communion with the Lord.

—CORA HARRIS MACILVARY

Remember...

Let never day nor night unhallowed pass,
but still remember what the Lord hath done.

—WILLIAM SHAKESPEARE

Cherish the Moment

Lord, help me to rejoice in the time I
have with my family today. I don't want to
dwell on what might happen in the future;
I want to relish this chance to nurture
and cherish the blessings You've given me.
Amen.

Sacred Beauty

She wore age so gracefully, so carelessly,
that there was a sacred beauty about her faded
cheek more lovely and lovable than all the
bloom of her youth. Happy [is the] woman
who [is] not afraid of growing old.

—DINAH MARIA MULOCK

Dreams

The tragedy of life doesn't lie in not reaching your goal. The tragedy lies in having no goal to reach. It isn't a calamity to die with dreams unfilled, but it is a calamity not to dream. It is not disgrace to not reach the stars, but it is a disgrace to have no stars to reach for.

—BENJAMIN MAYS

Catch the Trade Winds

Twenty years from now, you will be more
disappointed by the things you didn't do. So throw
off the bowlines. Sail away from the safe harbor.
Catch the trade winds in your sails.
Explore. Dream. Discover.

—MARK TWAIN

Respect

To have respect for ourselves guides our
morals; and to have deference for others
governs our manners.

—LAWRENCE STERNE

Teach

The aged women likewise, that they be in behavior
as becometh holiness, not false accusers,
not given to much wine, teachers of good things;
that they may teach the young women to be sober,
to love their husbands, to love their children,
to be discreet, chaste, keepers at home, good,
obedient to their own husbands.

—Titus 2:3–5 KJV

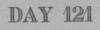

Opportunities

When one door closes, another one
opens; but we often look so long and
regretfully at the closed door that we fail
to see the one that has opened for us.

—ALEXANDER GRAHAM BELL

Soar!

Keep your feet on the ground, but let your heart soar as high as it will. Refuse to be average or to surrender to the chill of your spiritual environment.

—A. W. TOZER

The Right Question

I have. . .learned that when a baffling or painful experience comes, the crucial thing is not always to find the right answers, but to ask the right questions. . . . Often it is simply the right question at the right time that propels us into the journey of awakening.

—SUE MONK KIDD

Perfect Order

I used to think my house had to be in perfect order to invite a friend to tea. Now I realize we're very happy to be together in a dusty house with warm cookies.

—BONNIE JENSEN

The Unexpected

If one advances confidently in the
direction of his dreams and endeavors
to live the life which [she] has imagined,
[she] will meet with success unexpected
in common hours.

—HENRY DAVID THOREAU

Overcoming

Success is to be measured not so much by the
position that one has reached in life as by the
obstacles which [she] has overcome
trying to succeed.

—BOOKER T. WASHINGTON

Little Acts

That best portion of a good [woman's]
life, [her] little, nameless, unremembered
acts of kindness and love.

—WILLIAM WORDSWORTH

Be True To Yourself

This above all: To thine own self be true:
And it must follow as the night the day,
thou canst not then be false to any man.

—WILLIAM SHAKESPEARE

The Formula

I cannot give you the formula for success,
but I can give you the formula for failure,
which is: Try to please everybody.

—HERBERT B. SWOPE

Secure in Love

Lord, I know that bad things will come my way in
life, but I am secure in Your love that never fails.
I am constantly blessed by Your care and concern.
I am so important to You that even the hairs
of my head are all numbered. Amen.

Believe

When you come to the edge of all the light
you have and you must take a step into the
darkness of the unknown, believe that one
of two things will happen. Either there
will be something solid for you to stand
on—or you will be taught how to fly.

—PATRICK OVERTON

Character Development

Character cannot be developed in ease and quiet.
Only through experience of trial and suffering can
the soul be strengthened, vision cleared,
ambition inspired, and success achieved.

—HELEN KELLER

Passing Through

I expect to pass through this world but
once; any good thing therefore that I can
do, or any kindness that I can show to any
fellow-creature, let me do it now;
let me not defer or neglect it, for I shall
not pass this way again.

—ÉTIENNE DE GRELLET DU MABILLIER

Persistence

The heights by great men reached and kept
were not attained by sudden flight, but they,
while their companions slept, were toiling
upward in the night.

—HENRY WADSWORTH LONGFELLOW

DAY 135

Train Up a Child

Train up a child in the way he should go:
and when he is old, he will not
depart from it.

—PROVERBS 22:6 KJV

What Is Success?

Success is failure turned inside out—the silver tint
of the cloud of doubt—and you never can tell how
close you are, it may be near when it seems afar;
so stick to the fight when you're hardest hit—
it's when things seem worst that you must not quit.

—George Webster Douglas

Limitless Hope

When we take the time to notice the simple things in life, we never lack for encouragement. We discover we are surrounded by limitless hope that's just wearing everyday clothes.

—ANONYMOUS

Channels for Sharing

God has given us two hands—one to receive with
and the other to give with. We are not cisterns made
for hoarding; we are channels made for sharing.

—BILLY GRAHAM

Keep Love in Your Heart

Keep love in your heart. A life without it is like a sunless garden when the flowers are dead. The consciousness of loving and being loved brings a warmth and richness to life that nothing else can bring.

—OSCAR WILDE

Stand for Right

I am not bound to win, but I am bound to be
true. I am not bound to succeed, but I am bound
to live by the light that I have. I must stand with
anybody that stands right, stand with him while
he is right, and part [company] with him when
he goes wrong.

—ABRAHAM LINCOLN

Balance of Life

The best and safest thing is to keep a
balance in your life, acknowledge the
great powers around us and in us.
If you can do that, and live that way,
you are really a wise [woman].

—EURIPIDES

Truth in Your Word

Lord, let me know when I am wrong. That way I can come to You for cleansing and an opportunity to make things right. Thank You for the truth in Your Word, even though sometimes the truth hurts. Amen.

A Splendid Torch

Life is no brief candle to me. It is a sort
of splendid torch which I have got a hold
of for the moment, and I want to make
it burn as brightly as possible before
handing it on to future generations.

—GEORGE BERNARD SHAW

Keep On Trying

I am not judged by the number of times I fail,
but by the number of times I succeed; and the
number of times I succeed is in direct proportion to
the number of times I can fail and keep on trying.

—TOM HOPKINS

Take Notice

The wonderful thing about sunset,
and much the same can be said for sunrise,
is that it happens every day, and even if
the sunset itself is not spectacular,
it marks the beginning of another day.
It's a great time to pause and take notice.

—ELAINE ST. JAMES

The Wonder
of the World

I find each day too short for all the thoughts
I want to think, all the walks I want to take,
all the books I want to read, and all the friends
I want to see. The longer I live, the more
my mind dwells upon the beauty and
the wonder of the world.

—JOHN BURROUGHS

DAY 147

Small Pleasures

Happiness consists more in small
conveniences or pleasures that occur
every day, than in great pieces of good
fortune that happen but seldom to a
[woman] in the course of [her] life.

—BENJAMIN FRANKLIN

The Beauty of a Woman

The beauty of a woman is not in the clothes she wears, the figure that she carries, or the way she combs her hair. The beauty of a woman must be seen from in her eyes, because that is the doorway to her heart, and the place where love resides.

—AUDREY HEPBURN

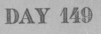

Profound Joy

Profound joy of the heart is like a magnet
that indicates the path of life. One has to
follow it, even though one enters into a
way full of difficulties.

—MOTHER TERESA

Trust in the Lord

Trust in the LORD with all thine heart; and lean not unto thine own understanding. In all thy ways acknowledge him, and he shall direct thy paths.

—PROVERBS 3:5–6 KJV

Press On

A new life begins for us with every
second. Let us go forward joyously to
meet it. We must press on, whether we
will or no, and we shall walk better with
our eyes before us than with them
ever cast behind.

—UNKNOWN

Good News

Everyone has inside of [her] a piece of good
news. The good news is that you don't know
how great you can be! How much you can love!
What you can accomplish!
And what your potential is!

—ANNE FRANK

Travel Light

The definition of traveling light may
vary from one individual to another.
But most of us need to trim off some
excess weight. We have too many social
involvements, an overabundance of good
but unnecessary meetings. . . . Remember
the caution: Beware of the barrenness
of a busy life.

—RUTH BELL GRAHAM

Pockets of Happiness

Between the house and the store there are little
pockets of happiness. A bird, a garden, a friend's
greeting, a child's smile, a cat in the sunshine
needing a stroke. Recognize them or ignore them.
It's always up to you.

—PAM BROWN

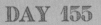

DAY 155

Gratitude

Gratitude consists in a watchful, minute
attention to the particulars of our state. . . .
It fills us with a consciousness that God
loves and cares for us, even to the least
event and smallest need of life.

—HENRY EDWARD MANNING

Two Ways to Live Life

There are only two ways to live your life.
One is as though nothing is a miracle.
The other is as though everything is a miracle.

—ALBERT EINSTEIN

Supreme Happiness

The supreme happiness of life is the
conviction of being loved for yourself or
more correctly being loved in spite
of yourself.

—VICTOR HUGO

Be Like a Bird

Be like the bird that, halting in its flight awhile
on boughs too slight, feels them give way beneath
her, and yet sings knowing that she hath wings.

—VICTOR HUGO

Bask in the Sunshine

Bask in the sunshine of [God's] love.
Drink of the waters of His goodness.
Keep your face upturned to Him as the
flowers do to the sun. Look, and your soul
shall live and grow.

—HANNAH WHITALL SMITH

The Sweetest Things in Life

The best things are nearest: breath in your nostrils,
light in your eyes, flowers at your feet, duties at
your hand, the path of Right just before you.
Do not grasp at the stars, but do life's plain
common work as it comes, certain that daily duties
and daily bread are the sweetest things in life.

—Robert Louis Stevenson

Be Alive To...

Life is what we are alive to. It is not
length but breadth.... Be alive to...
goodness, kindness, purity, love, history,
poetry, music, flowers, stars, God,
and eternal hope.

—MALTBIE D. BABCOCK

Love Produces Miracles

Love is the divine vitality that everywhere produces
and restores life. To each and every one of us,
it gives the power of working miracles if we will.

—LYDIA MARIA CHILD

Flow. . .

As your faith is strengthened you will find
that there is no longer the need to have
a sense of control, that things will flow
as they will, and that you will flow with
them, to your great delight and benefit.

—EMMANUEL TENEY

Be Patient

Be patient with everyone, but above all with
thyself. I mean, do not be disheartened by your
imperfections, but always rise up
with fresh courage.

—St. Francis de Sales

We Are His Workmanship

For we are his workmanship,
created in Christ Jesus unto good works,
which God hath before ordained that
we should walk in them.

—EPHESIANS 2:10 KJV

DAY 166

Heaven

To see a world in a grain of sand
And a heaven in a wildflower,
Hold infinity in the palm of your hand
And eternity in an hour.

—WILLIAM BLAKE

Miracle to Miracle

To be alive, to be able to see, to walk,
to have a home. . .friends—it's all a
miracle. I have adopted the technique of
living life from miracle to miracle.

—ARTHUR RUBENSTEIN

Faith Is the Root

Faith is the root of all blessings. Believe and you shall be saved; believe and your needs must be satisfied; believe and you cannot but be comforted and happy.

—JEREMY TAYLOR

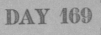

Believe and Follow

Far away there in the sunshine are my
highest aspirations. I may not reach them,
but I can look up and see their beauty,
believe in them, and try to follow
where they lead.

—LOUISA MAY ALCOTT

DAY 170

Today, Well Lived

Look to this day! For it is life, the very life of life. For yesterday is but a dream, and tomorrow is only a vision, but today well lived makes every yesterday a dream of happiness and tomorrow a vision of hope.

—KALIDASA

Feed Your Soul

The things we think on are the things
that feed our souls. If we think on pure
and lovely things, we shall grow pure and
lovely like them.

—HANNAH WHITALL SMITH

Renew My Commitment

Lord, I want to be instrumental in helping my
family establish a close walk with You. Direct me
daily to renew my commitment to follow in Your
steps. Thank You for being the example I need.
Amen.

DAY 173

Never Lose Sight

We may run, walk, stumble. . .or fly,
but let us never lose sight of the reason
for the journey or miss a chance to
see a rainbow on the way.

—GLORIA GAITHER

Embrace the Wonder

Embrace the wonder and excitement each day
brings. For tomorrow affords us new opportunities. . .
time to experience. . .time to create. . .
time to reflect. . .time to dream.

—K. WILLIAMS

DAY 175

Silence Is Required

There is so much noise in our modern
world that we may not at first realize how
much we need silence in order to hear. . . .
True conversation, even and especially
between those who love each other,
requires silence.

—NORVENE VEST

A New Day

Finish each day and be done with it.
You have done what you could; some blunders
and absurdities have crept in; forget them as
soon as you can. Tomorrow is a new day;
you shall begin it serenely and with too high
a spirit to be encumbered with
your old nonsense.

—RALPH WALDO EMERSON

Hold Fast to Dreams

Hold fast to dreams
For if dreams die
Life is a broken-winged bird
Afraid to fly.
Hold fast to dreams
For if dreams go
Life is a barren hill
Covered with snow.

—LANGSTON HUGHES

A Caring Friend

When we honestly ask ourselves which person in
our lives means the most to us, we often find that
it is those who instead of giving advice, solutions,
or cures, have chosen rather to share our pain and
touch our wounds with a warm and tender hand.
The friend who can be silent with us in a moment
of despair or confusion, who can stay with us in an
hour of grief and bereavement. Who can tolerate
not knowing, not curing, not healing, and face
with us the reality of our powerlessness,
that is a friend who cares.

—HENRI NOUWEN

Kindness

Guard well within yourself that treasure,
kindness. Know how to give without
hesitation, how to lose without regret,
how to acquire without meanness.

—GEORGE SAND

DAY 180

The Lord Bless Thee

The LORD bless thee, and keep thee: the LORD
make his face shine upon thee, and be gracious
unto thee: the LORD lift up his countenance upon
thee, and give thee peace.

—NUMBERS 6:24–26 KJV

Love Is Better

I hold it true, whate'er befall;
I feel it, when I sorrow most;
'Tis better to have loved and lost
Than never to have loved at all.

—ALFRED TENNYSON

Anonymous Benefits

There is no duty we so much underrate as the duty of being happy. By being happy, we sow anonymous benefits upon the world.

—ROBERT LOUIS STEVENSON

Enjoy Life

Is it so small a thing to have enjoyed the
sun, to have lived light in the spring,
to have loved, to have thought,
to have done?

—MATTHEW ARNOLD

DAY 184

Unending Praise

May your life become one glad and unending
praise to the Lord as you journey through this
world, and in the world that is to come!

—TERESA OF AVILA

A Lifetime

No matter what your age or your
condition, your dreams are renewable.
Whether you're 5 or 105, you have a
lifetime ahead of you!

—UNKNOWN

Basis for Living

The only basis for living is believing in life,
loving it, and applying the whole force of one's
intellect to know it better.

—EMILE ZOLA

God's Kindness

Be the living expression of God's
kindness: kindness in your face,
kindness in your eyes,
kindness in your smile.

—MOTHER TERESA

The Narrow Gate

Enter through the narrow gate. For wide is
the gate and broad is the road that leads to
destruction, and many enter through it.
But small is the gate and narrow the road
that leads to life, and only a few find it.

—MATTHEW 7:13–14 NIV

Today

No matter what looms ahead, if you can
eat today, enjoy today, mix good cheer
with friends today, enjoy it and
bless God for it.

—HENRY WARD BEECHER

Faith Is. . .

Faith is engaging in the deepest joy of heaven,
knowing [God's] unfathomable love for me as I
walk through the thorny desolate now.

—UNKNOWN

Kindness, Beauty, and Truth

The ideals that have lighted my way
and, time after time, have given me new
courage to face life cheerfully have been
kindness, beauty, and truth.
The trite subjects of human efforts,
possessions, outward success, [and] luxury
have always seemed to me contemptible.

—ALBERT EINSTEIN

Real Rest

Father, I need rest—rest from my schedule,
rest from the demands of my family, rest from
"doing" to a place of simply "being." Lead me to
that place. Calm my mind and my emotions so I
can slow down enough to find real rest. Amen.

God Answers

When the solution is simple,
God is answering.

—ALBERT EINSTEIN

Prayer

Do not pray for easy lives. Pray to be stronger.
Do not pray for tasks equal to your powers.
Pray for powers equal to your tasks.

—PHILLIPS BROOKS

Path of Life

Thou wilt shew me the path of life:
in thy presence is fulness of joy; at thy right
hand there are pleasures for evermore.

—Psalm 16:11 kjv

True Happiness

True happiness comes when we stop complaining
about all the troubles we have and offer thanks for
all the troubles we don't have.

—UNKNOWN

Truly Spiritual

We never become truly spiritual by sitting
down and wishing to become so.
You must undertake something so great
that you cannot accomplish it unaided.

—PHILLIPS BROOKS

A Grand Thing

It's such a grand thing to be a mother of a mother—that's why the world calls her grandmother.

—UNKNOWN

Moment by Moment

Let me tell thee, time is a very precious
gift from God; so precious that it's only
given to us moment by moment.

—AMELIA BARR

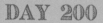

Real

Generally, by the time you are real, most of your hair has been loved off, and your eyes drop out and you get loose in the joints and very shabby. But these things don't matter at all, because once you are real you can't be ugly, except to people who don't understand.

—MARGERY WILLIAMS,
THE VELVETEEN RABBIT

A Matter of Choice

If becoming a grandmother was only a
matter of choice, I should advise every
one of you straightaway to become one.
There is no fun for old people like it!

—HANNAH WHITALL SMITH

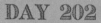

Elements of Joy

Into all our lives, in many simple, familiar, homely ways, God infuses this element of joy from the surprises of life, which unexpectedly brighten our days, and fill our eyes with light.

—HENRY WADSWORTH LONGFELLOW

Be Glad of Life

To be glad of life because it gives you the
chance to love and to work and to play
and to look up at the stars....to think...
often of your friends, and every day of
Christ...these are little guideposts
on the footpath of peace.

—HENRY VAN DYKE

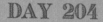

DAY 204

Words

Remember not only to say the right thing in the
right place, but far more difficult still, to leave
unsaid the wrong thing at the tempting moment.

—BENJAMIN FRANKLIN

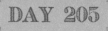

Three Important Things

Three things in human life are important:
The first is to be kind. The second is to
be kind. And the third is to be kind.

—HENRY JAMES

The Brightest Gems

Guard well your spare moments. They are like uncut diamonds. Discard them and their value will never be known. Improve them and they will become the brightest gems in a useful life.

—RALPH WALDO EMERSON

Our Distant Goal

It is for us to pray not for tasks equal to our powers, but for powers equal to our tasks, to go forward with a great desire forever beating at the door of our hearts as we travel toward our distant goal.

—HELEN KELLER

Every Day

Read, every day, something no one else is reading.
Think, every day, something no one else is
thinking. Do, every day, something no one else
would be silly enough to do. It is bad for the mind
to be always part of unanimity.

—CHRISTOPHER MORLEY

Keep Your Dreams

Keep thou thy dreams—the tissue of all
wings is woven first of them; from dreams
are made the precious and imperishable
things, whose loveliness lives on
and does not fade.

—VIRNA SHEARD

Seek the Lord

Seek the LORD and his strength, seek his face
continually. Remember his marvellous works that
he hath done, his wonders, and the judgments of
his mouth.

—1 CHRONICLES 16:11–12 KJV

A Keen Sense of Humor

A keen sense of humor helps us to overlook the unbecoming, understand the unconventional, tolerate the unpleasant, overcome the unexpected, and outlast the unbearable.

—BILLY GRAHAM

Real Hope

Lord, You are my hope in an often hopeless
world. You are my hope of heaven, my hope of
peace, my hope of change, purpose,
and unconditional love. Fill the reservoir of
my heart to overflowing with the joy that
real hope brings. Amen.

He Is Close Enough to Hear Us

We do not need to search for heaven, over here or over there, in order to find our eternal Father. In fact, we do not even need to speak out loud, for though we speak in the smallest whisper or the most fleeting thought, He is close enough to hear us.

—TERESA OF AVILA

A Startling Event

The miracles of nature do not seem miracles
because they are so common. If no one had ever
seen a flower, even a dandelion would be the most
startling event in the world.

—UNKNOWN

No Need

Where there is faith, there is love.
Where there is love, there is peace.
Where there is peace, there is God.
Where there is God, there is no need.

—UNKNOWN

Heaven's Glories

No coward soul is mine, no trembler in the world's
storm-troubled sphere: I see heaven's glories shine,
and faith shines equal arming me from fear.

—EMILY BRONTË

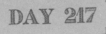

Home Sweet Home

Every house where love abides and
friendship is a guest, is surely home,
and home, sweet home, for there the
heart can rest.

—HENRY VAN DYKE

New Heights

When we move as God's hand guides us, safely under His wings, we will soar to new places and heights.

—SHERYL LYNN HILL

DAY 219

One Secret of Success

One secret of success in life is for a
[woman] to be ready for [her] opportunity
when it comes.

—BENJAMIN DISRAELI

Present Blessings

Reflect upon your present blessings, of which every
man has many, not on your past misfortunes,
of which all men have some.

—CHARLES DICKENS

To Serve

I don't know what your destiny will be but one thing I know: The only ones among you who will be really happy are those who sought and found how to serve.

—DR. ALBERT SCHWEITZER

Always Another Chance

If you have made mistakes, even serious ones,
there is always another chance for you. What we call
failure is not the falling down, but the staying down.

—MARY PICKFORD

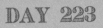

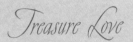

Treasure Love

Treasure the love you receive above all.
It will survive long after your gold and
good health have vanished.

—OG MANDINO

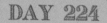

Part of the Plan

You are part of the plan, an indispensable part.
You are needed; you have your own unique
share in the freedom of Creation.

—MADELEINE L'ENGLE

Rejoice

But let all those that put their trust in
thee rejoice: let them ever shout for joy,
because thou defendest them: let them
also that love thy name be joyful in thee.

—PSALM 5:11 KJV

Evidence

Lord, there is so much I do not understand about You. Still, I can see the effects of Your actions, the evidence that You are still active in my daily life. I do not need to physically see You to believe Your evidence is everywhere. Amen.

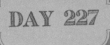

Beautiful

There is nothing Madison Avenue can give us that will make us more beautiful women. We are beautiful because God created us that way.

—MARIANNE WILLIAMSON

Take Time to Notice

I will take time to notice the good things when
they come. I will fix my mind on what is pure and
lovely and upright.

—ANITA CORRINE DONIHUE

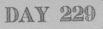

Happiness Comes from Within

Your happiness comes from within you,
not from the money you make, the trips
you take, or the things you own.

—FAITH STEWART

Be Confident

[Be] confident of this very thing, that he which hath begun a good work in you will perform it until the day of Jesus Christ.

—PHILIPPIANS 1:6 KJV

God Speaks

God whispers to us in our pleasures, speaks in our conscience, but shouts in our pains; it is His megaphone to rouse a deaf world.

—C. S. LEWIS

Trust

Father, as long as I trust in Your presence, I have
nothing to worry about. Nothing can separate me
from You, because You are the strong protector,
the mighty One who watches over me always.
I praise You, Lord, for Your protection. Amen.

A Grace

Our work is meant to be a grace. It is a
blessing and a gift, even a surprise and an
act of unconditional love toward
the community.

—MATTHEW FOX

The Inconsequential

Do not let trifles disturb your tranquility of
mind. . . . Life is too precious to be sacrificed
for the nonessential and transient. . . .
Ignore the inconsequential.

—GRENVILLE KLEISER

Live Your Life

When you were born, you cried and the world rejoiced. Live your life so that when you die, the world cries and you rejoice.

—CHEROKEE EXPRESSION

DAY 236

The Rock and the Stream

In the confrontation between the stream and the rock, the stream always wins—not through strength but by perseverance.

—H. Jackson Brown Jr.

Perfect Balance

So divinely is the world organized that
every one of us, in our place and time,
is in balance with everything else.

—JOHANN WOLFGANG VON GOETHE

New Hope

Each dawn holds a new hope for a new plan,
making the start of each day the start of a new life.

—GINA BLAIR

DAY 239

Meet Life

People grow through experience if they
meet life honestly and courageously.
This is how character is built.

—ELEANOR ROOSEVELT

DAY 240

Love Unselfishly

Love more persons more. . .more unselfishly,
without thought of return. The return, never fear,
will take care of itself.

—HENRY DRUMMOND

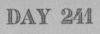
What God Knows

Reputation is what men and women think
of us; character is what God and angels
know of us.

—THOMAS PAINE

DAY 242

Great Faith

Little faith will bring your soul to heaven,
but great faith will bring heaven to your soul.

—CHARLES H. SPURGEON

Keep Your Face Toward God

Keep your face upturned to Him as the flowers do to the sun. Look, and your soul shall love and grow.

—HANNAH WHITALL SMITH

Hope Is Like the Sun

Hope is like the sun, which, as we journey toward it, casts the shadow of our burden behind us.

—SAMUEL SMILES

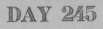

Real Joy

Real joy comes not from ease or riches or from the praise of men, but from doing something worthwhile.

—Sir Wilfred Grenfell

A Precious Ornament

You love the short, the impaired, those who
struggle with life and sometimes go under.
You love me, Lord, so much that You call me forth
by name and beautify me with Your salvation,
the most precious ornament I could ever wish for.
Amen.

By Work

I never did anything worth doing by
accident, nor did any of my inventions
come by accident; they came by work.

—THOMAS EDISON

God's Way

I am always content with what happens,
for I know that what God chooses is better
than what I choose.

—EPICTETUS

Grandma's House

Children, no matter what their age,
are always hungry when they go to
Grandma's house.

—UNKNOWN

A Right Heart

Great beauty, great strength, and great riches are
really and truly of no great use;
a right heart exceeds all.

—BENJAMIN FRANKLIN

The Happiest People

I think I began learning long ago that
those who are the happiest are those who
do the most for others.

—BOOKER T. WASHINGTON

What He Gives

Faith is the virtue by which clinging to the
faithfulness of God, we lean upon Him so that we
may obtain what He gives us.

—WILLIAM AMES

Sacrifice

The important thing is this: To be able at
any moment to sacrifice what we are for
what we could become.

—CHARLES DU BOIS

Quite Near

Have confidence in God's mercy,
for when you think He is a long way from you,
He is often quite near.

—THOMAS À KEMPIS

Let Your Light Shine

If you want your neighbor to see what the Christ Spirit will do for him, let him see what it has done for you.

—HENRY WARD BEECHER

Big Difference

Your attitude about who you are and what you have
is a very little thing that makes
a very big difference.

—THEODORE ROOSEVELT

A Little Relaxation

Every now and then go away, have a little
relaxation; for when you come back to
your work, your judgment will be surer.

—LEONARDO DA VINCI

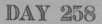

God Is Sufficient

Let nothing disturb you, let nothing frighten you:
everything passes away except God;
God alone is sufficient.

—TERESA OF AVILA

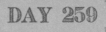

Peace and Joy

Where the soul is full of peace and joy,
outward surroundings and circumstances
are of comparatively little account.

—HANNAH WHITALL SMITH

DAY 260

Blessed Promise

Father, physically I'm wearing out. But in the core of my being, in my heart, I still feel strengthened by You. What a blessed promise that this inner strength will by my portion forever. Amen.

Love Divine, All Loves Excelling

Love divine, all loves excelling,
Joy of heaven to earth come down;
Fix in us Thy humble dwelling;
All Thy faithful mercies crown!
Jesus, Thou art all compassion,
Pure unbounded love Thou art;
Visit us with Thy salvation;
Enter every trembling heart.

—CHARLES WESLEY

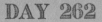

The Miracle of Love

This is one of the miracles of love: It gives. . .
a power of seeing through its own enchantments
and yet not being disenchanted.

—C. S. LEWIS

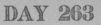
The Birthday of a King

'Twas a humble birthplace,
but O how much God gave to us that day,
From the manger bed what a path has led,
what a perfect, holy way.
Alleluia! O how the angels sang.
Alleluia! How it rang!
And the sky was bright with a holy light
'Twas the birthday of a King.

—WILLIAM H. NEIDLINGER

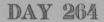

Duty

Let us have faith that right makes might,
and in that faith let us to the end dare to do
our duty as we understand it.

—ABRAHAM LINCOLN

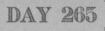

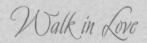

Walk in Love

And walk in love, as Christ also hath
loved us, and hath given himself for us an
offering and a sacrifice to God for a
sweet-smelling savor.

—EPHESIANS 5:2 KJV

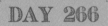

Treasures

Memories are the treasures that we keep locked
deep within the storehouse of our souls, to keep
our hearts warm when we are lonely.

—BECKY ALIGADA

The Best You Can

There's a thing to remember: that you
don't belong to yourself at all and are
bound to do the best you can with your
time and strength and everything.

—GRACE LIVINGSTON HILL

The Good Side of Things

Nothing contributes more to cheerfulness than the
habit of looking at the good side of things.
The good side is God's side of them.

—W. B. Ullathorne

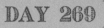

Age Is Opportunity

For age is opportunity no less than youth
itself, though in another dress.
And as the evening twilight fades away,
The sky is filled with stars invisible by day.

—HENRY WADSWORTH LONGFELLOW

Grace Is Sufficient

But he said to me, "My grace is sufficient for
you, for my power is made perfect in weakness."
Therefore I will boast all the more gladly about my
weaknesses, so that Christ's power may rest on me.

—2 CORINTHIANS 12:9 NIV

Amazing Grace

Thro' many dangers, toils, and snares,
I have already come;
'Tis grace hath brought me safe thus far,
And grace will lead me home.

—JOHN NEWTON

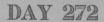

Until Morning

Make sure you never, never argue at night.
You just lose a good night's sleep, and you can't
settle anything until morning anyway.

—ROSE KENNEDY
(ADVICE TO HER FIRST MARRIED
GRANDDAUGHTER)

Travel

It is God to whom and with whom we travel, and while He is the End of our journey, He is also at every stopping place.

—Elisabeth Eliot

Tenderness and Respect

When I approach a child, he inspires in me two
sentiments; tenderness for what he is,
and respect for what he may become.

—LOUIS PASTEUR

He Is Praying

If I could hear Christ praying for me
in the next room, I would not fear a
million enemies. Yet distance makes no
difference, He is praying for me.

—ROBERT MURRAY MCCHEYNE

*The Sweet
Simple Things of Life*

I am beginning to learn that it is the sweet,
simple things of life which are the real ones after all.

—Laura Ingalls Wilder

Achieving

The greatest satisfaction in life is achieving
what everyone said could not be done.

—CHINESE PROVERB

Sixty
Minutes an Hour

The future is something which everyone
reaches at the rate of sixty minutes an hour,
whatever he does, whoever he is.

—C. S. Lewis

Eternal Blessings

Father, Your correction lasts only a
moment; but its blessings are eternal.
When I realize You are so concerned for
me and want to help me, I am filled with
gratitude and willing to be led in the right
direction. Amen.

Kindness Spoken

A little word in kindness spoken,
A motion or a tear,
Has often healed the heart that's broken
And made a friend sincere.

—D. C. COLESWORTHY

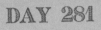

Enjoy Today

Don't put off for tomorrow what you can
do today; because if you enjoy it today,
you can do it again tomorrow.

—JAMES A. MICHENER

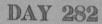

Surrender the Moment

If you surrender completely to the moments as they pass, you live more richly those moments.

—ANNE MORROW LINDBERGH

Hope Is a Light

Hope, like the gleaming taper's light,
adorns and cheers our way;
and still, as darker grows the night,
emits a lighter ray.

—OLIVER GOLDSMITH

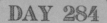

Two Things

There are two things one should know
about the direction of (her) life.
First is: Where am I going?
Second is: Who will go with me?

—ELIE WIESEL

Every Gift Is from Above

Every good and perfect gift is from above,
coming down from the Father of the
heavenly lights, who does not change like
shifting shadows.

—JAMES 1:17 NIV

The Harvest

Talk unbelief, and you will have unbelief;
talk faith, and you will have faith. According to
the seed sown will be the harvest.

—PLATO

Eternally Secure

And none shall pluck us from that hand.
Eternally we are secure. Though heaven
and earth shall pass away, [God's] word
forever shall endure.

—Mrs. M. E. Rae

Becoming a Grandmother

Becoming a grandmother is wonderful.
One moment you're just a mother, the next you're
all wise and prehistoric.

—PAM BROWN

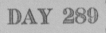

Small Things

Faith in small things has repercussions
that ripple all the way out. In a huge,
dark room a little match can
light up a place.

—JONI EARECKSON TADA

DAY 290

Teach Me to Focus

Lord, I ask for Your help when it comes to
getting along with my family members.
Teach me to focus on the good times we had
together, not the bad, and to concentrate on
their good points for the sake of family
peace. Amen.

Cheerfulness

The cheerful live the longest in years,
and afterward in our regards.
Cheerfulness is the offshoot of goodness.

—CHRISTIAN NESTELL BOVÉE

Ordinary Acts

The ordinary acts we practice every day at home
are of more importance to the soul than their
simplicity might suggest.

—THOMAS MORE

A Unique Role

Everyone has a unique role to fill in
the world and is important in some
respect. Everyone, including and perhaps
especially you, is indispensable.

—NATHANIAL HAWTHORNE

Faith and Goodness

The unwarped child, with his spontaneous faith
and confidence in goodness, is the best illustration
of that spirit which fits the Kingdom of God.

—RUFUS M. JONES

Optimism

Love is optimistic; it looks at people in
the best light. Love thinks constructively
as it senses the grand possibilities in
other people.

—GEORGE SWEETING

Christianity Is a Living Process

Christianity is not a theory or speculation,
but a life; not a philosophy of life, but a life
and a living process.

—SAMUEL TAYLOR COLERIDGE

Miracles Can Happen

When we accept tough jobs as a challenge
and wade into them with joy and
enthusiasm, miracles can happen.

—ARLAND GILBERT

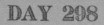

Grandmother

Grandmother—a wonderful mother
with lots of patience.

—UNKNOWN

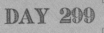

Human Love

Human love and the delights of
friendship, out of which are built the
memories that endure, are also to be
treasured up as hints of what
shall be hereafter.

—BEDE JARETT

Enchanted

A mother becomes a true grandmother the day she stops noticing the terrible things her children do because she is so enchanted with the wonderful things her grandchildren do.

—LOIS WYSE

Handful of Stars

If I could reach up and hold a star for
every time you've made me smile,
the entire evening sky would be in the
palm of my hand.

—UNKNOWN

Double Delight

To show a child what has once delighted you, to
find the child's delight added to your own,
so that there is now a double delight seen in the
glow of trust and affection, this is happiness.

—J. B. PRIESTLEY

The Heart Has Its Own Memory

The heart has its own memory like the
mind, and in it are enshrined the precious
keepsakes, into which is wrought the
giver's loving thought.

—HENRY WADSWORTH LONGFELLOW

As the Angels Give

If instead of a gem, or even a flower, we could cast the gift of a lovely thought into the heart of a friend, that would be giving as the angels give.

—GEORGE MACDONALD

Spiritual Growth

Lord, I really want to grow spiritually.
I need to—for my own daily walk with
You and, most importantly, because
You've commanded me to. Thank You
for giving me the strength to fulfill Your
commands and to grow spiritually. Amen.

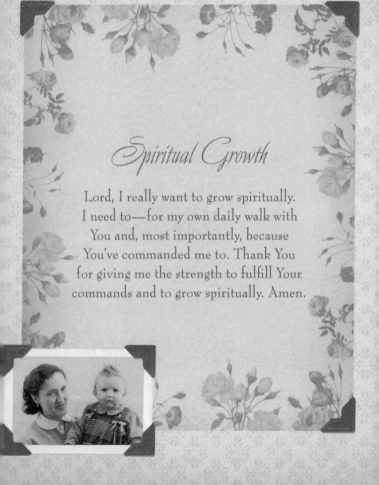

Grandmas Hold Our Hearts Forever

Grandmas hold our tiny hands for just a little
while. . .but our hearts forever.

—Unknown

When Things Are Complicated

When things are complicated,
I wish you simple beauty;
When things are chaotic,
I wish you inner peace;
When things seem empty,
I wish you hope and joy.

—ANONYMOUS

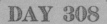

Sing!

Optimism is the cheerful frame of mind that
enables a teakettle to sing, though in hot water
up to its nose.

—ANONYMOUS

Long on Love

Grandmother-grandchild relationships
are simple. Grandmas are short on
criticism and long on love.

—UNKNOWN

Forgive and Forget

Forgive, forget. Bear with the faults of others as
you would have them bear with yours.
Be patient and understanding.

—PHILLIPS BROOKS

Masterpieces

Grandmothers and roses are much the same. Each are God's masterpieces with different names.

—UNKNOWN

Unexpected Sparks

Pleasure is very seldom found where it is sought.
Our brightest blazes are commonly kindled by
unexpected sparks.

—SAMUEL JOHNSON

A Splendid Gift

Live your life while you have it. Life is a
splendid gift—there is nothing
small about it.

—Florence Nightingale

Words of Wisdom

It is good to have an end to journey toward; but it is the journey that matters in the end.

—URSULA K. LEGUIN

Health: To eat what you don't want, drink what you don't like, and do what you'd rather not.

—MARK TWAIN

Unless someone like you cares a whole awful lot, nothing is going to get better. It's not.

—DR. SEUSS

Blessed

And blessed is she that believed: for there
shall be a performance of those things
which were told her from the Lord.

—LUKE 1:45 KJV

Compensation

Grandchildren are God's compensation for
gray hair and wrinkles.

—UNKNOWN

Beauty Is God's Handwriting

Never lose an opportunity of seeing
anything that is beautiful; for beauty is
God's handwriting.

—RALPH WALDO EMERSON

Mount Up with Wings

Our enemies may build a wall around us as high as they please, but they cannot build any barrier between us and God; and if we "mount up with wings," we can fly higher than any of their walls can ever reach.

—HANNAH WHITALL SMITH

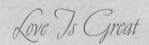

Love Is Great

Love is a great thing, an altogether good
gift, the only thing that makes burdens
light and bears all that is hard with ease.
It carries a weight without feeling it and
makes all that is bitter sweet and pleasant
to the taste.

—THOMAS À KEMPIS

Share the Gift

Heavenly Father, my greatest responsibility as
Your child is to share the gift of salvation with
others. My family, my neighbors, my children—
so many people need to hear Your Word.
Make me attentive to each opportunity
You present to me. Amen.

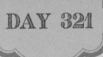

Immortal

Our Creator would never have made such
lovely days, and have given us the deep
hearts to enjoy them, above and beyond
all thought, unless we were
meant to be immortal.

—NATHANIAL HAWTHORNE

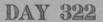

Greatest Pleasures

Do you know that conversation is one of the
greatest pleasures in life?

—W. SOMERSET MAUGHAM

If Love Were What the Rose Is

If love were what the rose is,
And I were like the leaf,
Our lives would grow together
In sad or singing weather,
Blown fields or flowerful closes,
Green pleasure or gray grief;
If love were as the rose is,
And I were like the leaf.

—ALGERNON CHARLES SWINBURNE

The Happy Glow

The happy glow that sharing brings,
A secret smile, a small surprise,
A special look in a loved one's eyes.
Comfort given, interest shown,
Quiet moments spent alone—
It's the "little things," small and sweet,
That make loving so complete.

—UNKNOWN

A Thing of Beauty

A thing of beauty is a joy forever:
Its loveliness increases; it will never
pass unto nothingness. . . . An endless
fountain of immortal drink,
pouring unto us from heaven's brink.

—JOHN KEATS

DAY 326

Unnecessary Burdens

Unnecessary possessions are unnecessary
burdens. If you have them, you have to
take care of them! There is great freedom
in simplicity of living. It is those who have
enough but not too much who
are the happiest.

—PEACE PILGRIM

Counting Memories

When we start to count flowers,
we cease to count weeds;
When we start to count blessings,
we cease to count needs;
When we start to count laughter,
we cease to count tears;
When we start to count memories,
we cease to count years.

—ANONYMOUS

A Work of Grace

The cry of a young raven is nothing but the natural
cry of a creature; but your cry, if it be sincere,
is the result of a work of grace in your heart.

—CHARLES H. SPURGEON

Rest

Rest is not idleness, and to lie sometimes
on the grass under trees on a summer's
day, listening to the murmur of the water
or watching the clouds float across the
sky, is by no means a waste of time.

—JOHN LUBBOCK

Press Toward the Mark

Brethren, I count not myself to have apprehended:
but this one thing I do, forgetting those things
which are behind, and reaching forth unto those
things which are before, I press toward the mark for
the prize of the high calling of God in Christ Jesus.

—PHILIPPIANS 3:13–14 KJV

There Is Beauty

There is beauty in the forest
when the trees are green and fair,
There is beauty in the meadow
when the wildflowers scent the air.
There is beauty in the sunlight
and the soft blue beams above.
Oh, the world is full of beauty
when the heart is full of love.

—UNKNOWN

Praises

The sun. . .in its full glory, either at rising or
setting—this, and many other like blessings we
enjoy daily; and for the most of them,
because they are so common, most men forget
to pay their praises. But let not us.

—IZAAK WALTON

DAY 333

On the Run

Half the joy of life is in little things taken
on the run. Let us run if we must. . .
but let us keep our hearts young and our
eyes open that nothing worth our while
shall escape us. And everything is worth
its while if we only grasp it
and its significance.

—CHARLES VICTOR CHERBULIEZ

Grace

Grace, 'tis a charming sound, harmonious to mine ear; heaven with the echo shall resound, and all the earth shall hear. Grace first contrived the way to save rebellious man; and all the steps that grace display which drew the wondrous plan.

—PHILIP DODDRIDGE

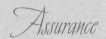

Assurance

Father, I can't begin to count the number
of times You've wrapped Your loving arms
around me and calmed me in the midst
of fears. You've drawn me near in times of
sorrow and given me assurance when I've
faced great disappointment. Amen.

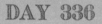

To Be Alive

How beautiful it is to be alive! To wake each
morn as if the Maker's grace did us a fresh from
nothingness derive, that we might sing "How happy
is our case! How beautiful it is to be alive!"

—HENRY SEPTIMUS SUTTON

Tranquility

In the forest we can rise above our
worldly care; in the forest we may find
tranquility and share the silence and
the secret strength of great and ancient
trees—sturdy oaks and silver birches,
laughing in the breeze.

—PATIENCE STRONG

DAY 338

Our Enjoyment

Trust should be in God, who richly gives us
all we need for our enjoyment.

—1 Timothy 6:17 NLT

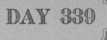

The Root of All Things

The wonder of living is held within the
beauty of silence, the glory of sunlight,
the sweetness of fresh spring air, the quiet
of strength of earth, and the love that lies
at the very root of all things.

—ANONYMOUS

My Crown

My crown is in my heart, not on my head,
not decked with diamonds and Indian stones,
nor to be seen; my crown is called content;
a crown it is that seldom kings enjoy.

—WILLIAM SHAKESPEARE, HENRY VI

Set Our Hearts Right

To put the world in order, we must first
put the nation in order. To put the nation
in order, we must first put the family in
order. To put the family in order,
we must first cultivate our personal life.
And to cultivate our personal life,
we must set our hearts right.

—CONFUCIUS

Seize the Moment

Seize the moment of excited curiosity on any
subject to solve your doubts; for if you let it pass,
the desire may never return.

—WILLIAM WIRT

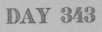

Loved

Women wish to be loved without a
why or wherefore, not because they are
pretty, or good, or well-bred, or graceful,
or intelligent, but because they are
themselves.

—Henri Frederic Amiel

My Heart

My heart is like a singing bird
whose nest is in a water'd shoot;
My heart is like an apple-tree
whose boughs are bent with thick-set fruit;
My heart is like rainbow shell
that paddles in a halcyon sea;
My heart is gladder than all these,
Because my love is come to me.

—CHRISTINA ROSSETTI

My Helper

Let your conversation be without
covetousness; and be content with such
things as ye have: for he hath said,
I will never leave thee, nor forsake thee.
So that we may boldly say, The Lord is
my helper, and I will not fear
what man shall do unto me.

—HEBREWS 13:5–6 KJV

Those Who Love

Those who love are borne on wings; they run and are filled with joy; they are free and unrestricted. . . . Beyond all things they rest in the one highest thing, from Whom streams all that is good.

—THOMAS À KEMPIS

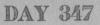

Thankfulness

I thank You, God, for this most amazing
day, for the leaping greenly spirits of
trees, and for the blue dream of sky and
for everything which is natural which is
infinite, which is yes.

—E. E. Cummings

Flying Power

We can surely accept with thankfulness every trial that compels us to use our wings, for only so they can grow strong and large and fit for the highest flying. Unused wings gradually wither and shrink and lose their flying power.

—HANNAH WHITALL SMITH

Hidden Delight

The world is so full of care and sorrow
that it is a gracious debt we owe to one
another to discover the bright crystals of
delight hidden in somber circumstances
and irksome tasks.

—HELEN KELLER

Grant Me Understanding

Lord, as I read and study Your Word and hear
sermons preached about it, I still have questions
and much to learn. I ask that You give me a
clear understanding of what You are saying
to me through it. Amen.

God's Grace

God's grace is too big, too great to understand fully. So we must take the moments of His grace throughout the day with us; the music of the songbird in the morning, the kindness shown in the afternoon, and the restful sleep at night.

—ANONYMOUS

Let Beauty Awake

Let beauty awake in the morn
from beautiful dreams,
Beauty awake from rest!
Let beauty awake
For beauty's sake
In the hour when the birds awake in the brake
And the stars are bright in the west!

—ROBERT LOUIS STEVENSON

The Gift of Grace

Like any other gift, the gift of grace can
be yours only if you'll reach out and take
it. Maybe being able to reach out and take
it is a gift, too.

—FREDERICK BUECHNER

Cherish. . .

Cherish your visions, cherish your ideals;
cherish the music that stirs in your heart, the
beauty that forms in your mind, the loveliness that
drapes your purest thoughts, for out of them will grow
all delightful conditions, all heavenly environment.

—James Allen

Short Steps

Most of the people who will walk after me
will be children, so make the beat keep
time with short steps.

—HANS CHRISTIAN ANDERSEN

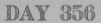

Grace Is Available

Grace is available for each of us every day. . .
but we've got to remember to ask for it with a
grateful heart and not to worry about whether
there will be enough for tomorrow.

—SARAH BAN BREATHNACH

Magic Mirrors

Family faces are magic mirrors.
Looking at people who belong to us, we
see the past, present, and future.

—GAIL LUMET BUCKLEY

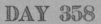

Grace Shall Abound

No one was ever saved because his sins were
small; no one was ever rejected on account of the
greatness of his sins. Where sin abounded,
grace shall much more abound.

—ARCHIBALD ALEXANDER

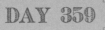

Enjoyment

You must not know too much or be too precise or scientific about birds and trees and flowers and water craft; a certain free margin, and even vagueness—perhaps ignorance, credulity—helps your enjoyment of these things.

—WALT WHITMAN

Passing by Happiness

Sometimes our thoughts turn back toward a corner
in a forest, or the end of a bank, or an orchard
filled with flowers, seen but a single time. . .
yet remaining in our hearts. . .a feeling [we]
have just passed by happiness.

—GUY DE MAUPASSANT

I Long For...

I long for scenes where man has never trod; a place where woman never smil'd or wept; there to abide with my creator, God. And sleep as I in childhood sweetly slept; untroubling and untroubled where I lie; the grass below—above the vaulted sky.

—JOHN CLARE

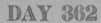

DAY 362

Free Grace

Grace is free, but when once you take it you are
bound forever to the giver, and bound to catch
the spirit of the giver. Like produces like, grace
makes you gracious, the giver makes you give.

—E. STANLEY JONES

The Spur of Delights

The imagination is the spur of delights. . .
all depend upon it, it is the mainspring of
everything; now, it is not by means of the
imagination one knows joy?
It is not of the imagination that the
sharpest pleasures arise?

—Marquis de Sade

Love Is an Image of God

Love is an image of God, and not a lifelong image, but the living essence of the divine nature which beams full of all goodness.

—MARTIN LUTHER

DAY 365

My Anchor Holds

And it holds, my anchor holds;
Blow your wildest then, O gale,
On my bark so small and frail,
By His grace I shall not fail,
For my anchor holds,
My anchor holds.

—W. C. MARTIN

NOTES

NOTES

NOTES

NOTES

NOTES

NOTES

NOTES

NOTES

NOTES

_____

_____

_____

_____

_____

_____

_____

_____

_____

_____

_____

_____

_____

NOTES

NOTES

_____

_____

_____

_____

_____

_____

_____

_____

_____

_____

_____

_____

_____

NOTES

NOTES

NOTES

NOTES

_____

_____

_____

_____

_____

_____

_____

_____

_____

_____

_____

_____

_____

_____